It's Time To Make A Living

Family - Fun - Finances

Written by
Erick G. Benson

Back word
By
DeJoiré C. Benson

First published by Dog Ear Publishing
4010 W. 86th Street, Ste H
Indianapolis, IN 46268
www.dogearpublishing.net

ISBN: 978-159858-823-1

This book is printed on acid-free paper.

Printed in the United States of America

Acknowledgements

I know clearly from where my blessings flow. The Lord has truly blessed me with the ability to express myself through the written word.

Thank you so much **mom**, for providing me with a great upbringing. I thank my father, who is now in heaven, for the great example that he illustrated in my life.

Thank you to my wife, **DeJoiré**, for all your love and support through this wonderful book venture. I thank you for your contributions as well.

To **Ericka** and **Déja**, you are truly the best daughters in the world.

Thank you to **Doris Williams** (mother-in-law) for being one of my proofreaders.

Thank you, **Deborah Bradley**, for taking the time to review my manuscript. I truly value your opinion.

To **Pastor Chuck Singleton** and **First Lady**, **Charlyn Singleton**, thank you for your continued prayers and leadership.

Thank you, **Terrell Hickman**, for your tremendous financial planning and investment advice as well as your tips for this book.

Thank you, **Kevin Copeland**, for reading my manuscript from a CEO's point of view.

Oscar, **Dorothy**, **Steve**, and **Kim Manning**, thank you so much for keeping all of my writing projects in your prayers.

Thank you, **Rose Dade**, for your daily prayers and encouragement for all my writing projects.

To **Sam Randolph**, **Sherie Crichlow**, **Anthony Herron**, and **Brandon Richardson,** thank you for your continued support that you have shown to my family and I.

To my **brothers**, **sisters**, **cousins**, **extended family** and **close friends** and **co-workers**, I thank you so much for your continued support.

To my business mentors—whether you were able to lend your support, give a special word of inspiration, or if you simply provided great leadership—your efforts and friendship are priceless:

Robert & Darcelle Wesley, Donald & Deborah Bradley, Keenith & Mendi Reed, Calvin Ellerbe, Roderick Houston, Spencer Iverson, Floyd Williams, Melissa Boston,

Chaurice Corbin, Larease Rivers, Jil Greene, Lynda Ward, Andria Hall and Katrina Greenhill. In addition, I would like to give a special thanks to Kim Sorenson, Scott Tomer and the "Coach", J. Lloyd Tomer. You three men have been a blessing to my family and I as well as to thousands upon thousands of families across the country.

Introduction

I am not a Harvard graduate, nor did I attend Stanford or MIT. Matter of fact, I grew up in Compton, California as a young kid. As a teenager, I attended Lynwood High School and I was a 'B' average student and a star athlete in baseball and football. My high school interception record still stands today. But, the real gift and blessing was the privilege of having a mom and dad at home to raise me and my brothers and sisters. A warm home, food on the table and a Godly upbringing does have its advantages. And by the way, I did go to college, though it was a state college mind you, but I believe the work is all the same. I even went on to earn a masters degree from a small college. The lesson I learned was that no matter where I earned my degrees, I still had to make my own way. There were no silver platters handed out with the degrees. I had to put in work, whether it was in school or business. The bottom line is, I'm just a down-to- earth guy with some basic business information to pass on to those who care to listen. It has been said that, "Those who bother to listen can sometimes lessen their load." I don't think that anyone famous said that, but it sounds good to me. This book is meant to inform you of brilliant avenues in which to make a living as well as to share basic business advice. There is daily proof and valid testimony on the advantages of creating or acquiring an internet-based business as well as a home-based business that can be one in the same. I will present samples as well as ideas on my personal take on why certain businesses are the wave of the future. Sometimes a little advice can change your life. It simply takes a bit of faith to step out of your comfort zone. Home-based businesses and the internet are surely not the only method to make a good living, but they are certainly proven ways.

No matter what you may think or believe regarding my ability or qualifications to write this book, the proof is in the pudding, listening works. The facts are the facts, and basic business principals do work for my family. There is no better experience than to live through the opportunity that you are presenting to others.

Some of your biggest critics and potential haters are your own family members, not to mention so-called good friends.

That may be unfortunate, but it is true all the same. The key is that you must keep on keeping on no matter what obstacles get in the way. Even when you are hurting and emotionally drained, you must keep your eyes on the prize.

I've learned to use people's anger and jealousy as fuel for my creative and business juices to flow. When you actually decide to go for what you want, no one can stop you. Especially, if you put God first, there is no way you can lose.

This is a simple book, with true information, about basic practices that work for me and my family.

I don't get caught up on anyone's titles and I am not impressed with someone's knowledge and/or riches unless they are willing to share their thoughts and testimony with others.

I'm just a common man with a simple plan regarding basic business.

Just A Thought

My pastor, Chuck Singleton, left a particular quote from a famous person on his cellular voice message for several weeks, and I enjoyed listening to it every time I heard the words.

"Don't depend on your eyes, when your imagination is out of focus." (Mark Twain)

I guess it's true that negative people really do hurt themselves more than others, when they attempt to spread negativity. Don't ever allow negative people to thwart your dreams or to discourage you from moving forward on an idea. It is better to encourage than to criticize with no merit. So yes, we should do unto others as we would want done unto ourselves. Wouldn't the world really and truly be a better place?

* **Scott** and **Felicia Jones,** your **positive demeanor** and **encouragement** mean the world to me.

Preface

I purposely wrote a short book, because I have learned over the years that some people don't read a lot. People will start a book and not finish it, or if a book is not immediately captivating, they won't give the book the time of day to complete it. For those of you who are avid readers, I wanted to ensure that this book was a quick read, so it would not interfere with the book that you are currently reading. I do believe this book can add some light to your path no matter what road of finances you may be traveling on in life.

As the old folks used to say in church, "Make it plain," and in this book, I definitely make the information plain.

Table of Contents

Excuses…Excuses…Excuses

Excuses are the intangible obstacles, which keep thousands upon thousands of individuals from ever becoming successful in business.

****

Question???

(Please answer the following question at the conclusion of this book)

Scenario: If you had an existing business that had the potential to make you money but societal woes caused a slowdown in the income being generated, would you simply quit your business? On the other hand, would you continue to pay the necessary fees for the cost of doing business, with the hope that your business will make a considerable amount of money in the future?

Clues: A- Cable television, acrylic nails, golf, dining out, shopping sprees, the movies

B- Residual income, generational wealth, tax incentives, time management

Do not answer the question until you read the entire book

1

Liberty for All

Liberty is the quality or state of being free, the power to do what one pleases, the positive enjoyment of various social, political, or economical rights and privileges as well as the power of choice. These are some of the eloquent descriptions of liberty, provided by the Merriam-Webster's Collegiate Dictionary. In the world of business, liberty is not an automatic platform for the typical person that works 9 to 5. However, liberty in the business world can be obtained for many who choose to go into business for themselves.

America is definitely the land of the free and the brave and the place where liberty should be for all. America is also the place where opportunities are as prevalent as falling rain and a land that oftentimes delivers phenomenal dreams, if pursued properly. Unfortunately, not everyone in America experiences the joy of living the American dream. Some people miss their dream due to circumstances, while others do not realize that their American dream is right in front of them for the taking. There may be several definitions for the American dream, but for the purposes of this book, I believe that living the American dream is captured in the manner of how you spend your time. I believe that time is priceless and only you can apply its true value in accordance with your lifestyle. Where do you spend the majority of your time? Do you spend the majority of your time working for an employer? Do you spend the majority of your time fellowshipping and enjoying your family? Do you spend the majority of your time worrying about money issues and fulfilling the basic needs in life? Have you really ever thought about how you spend the majority of your time?

If you had no time constraints, combined with a multitude of money, what would you do? Would you go on lavish vacations, would you sit at home and write a best selling novel, or would you go on the ultimate shopping spree? Of course, only you can answer that question. There are people throughout America that have lots of time and plenty of money to do whatever they choose to do on any given day. Can you imagine such a lifestyle? Some people have taken advantage of their opportunities and created enormous amounts of wealth. By doing so, they do live their American dream. The truth of the matter is that people in America, as well as in other parts of the world, are living under various circumstances. Some people have ready-made opportunities and access to wealth, while others have to create their own opportunities to have the chance to acquire wealth. I do not believe there will ever be a way to level the monetary playing field, but I do believe there is a way to create opportunities for all people who desire to live their American dream.

Let's face the facts, many people may have a desire to improve their financial situation, but if they do not have the necessary resources, their chances for personal improvement are highly diminished. If you desire to experience your own American dream, I do believe that true liberty is available for you at minimal risk. Your biggest risk in life is doing nothing. Nothing from nothing leaves nothing, right?

Conventional wisdom would have you believe that it is okay for you to work for a company and continue to contribute to that company's wealth. Your personal time is at risk and your employer continues to control the amount of funds that you earn.

A good friend told me he read that multi-millionaire Donald Trump, stated that if one day he were left with nothing, the first thing he would do to re-gain wealth is to seek a network marketing opportunity. Yes, he said it and I agree with him. Trump hit the nail right on the head.

The beauty of network marketing is that you can truly control your own destiny. You make the rules and you guide your own way to success. Don't believe the hype, network marketing is fun and financially rewarding and you control your time. Network marketing is actually an opportunity to create your own opportunity for years to come.

Liberty for all can truly be found through network marketing as you have the ability to create tremendous wealth for yourself. Individuals who speak negatively regarding network marketing simply do so, because they do not understand the dynamics behind the opportunity. Nevertheless, the very same people that speak negatively about network marketing are some of the biggest network marketers in the world and they don't even realize it. Case in point, all the times that you open your mouth and share information about the great restaurant where you ate, that good movie you saw, that sharp outfit you just bought and the breathtaking trip you recently took, you have fully participated in network marketing and didn't get paid a dime. Whether you want to admit it or not, you are an unpaid, network-marketing representative.

Some folks regard network marketing as a pyramid, or some other type of illegal entity. A typical pyramid scheme is displayed as a business venture without a product. A pyramid could also be an opportunity with a product that is overpriced for its market value, in order to be able to compensate a potential down line of clients. Moreover, as far as alignment, America's corporate setting is structured more in the form of a pyramid, which I will demonstrate in a latter chapter.

I believe beyond a shadow of a doubt that network marketing is the great financial equalizer. You do not need thousands of dollars to create your own opportunity, which I will also cover in detail in a latter chapter. Network marketing is the opportunity that can level the financial playing field. You cannot afford not to take advantage of this type of opportunity. No matter what your financial status or circumstances may be, a network marketing opportunity can change your life.

Caution: You will experience pitfalls along the way as you operate your network marketing business. There is no smooth road on your journey to the top. There will be adversity, frustration, negativity, disappointment, jealousy, and rejection. At the end of the day, the solution to any of the pre-mentioned problems is to keep networking and don't ever quit.

The remaining chapters in this book will touch on various topics and issues that Americans contend with in some form or fashion on a daily basis. Now, I urge you to sit back, relax and enjoy reading the remaining chapters.

I'm just a common man with a simple plan.

2

Working 9 to 5 To Make A Living

Ms. Dolly Parton, sang the words so brilliantly, "Working 9 to 5, what a way to make a living." Yes, it is a way but of course, it is not the only way. Working 9 to 5 is a time-consuming way, it is a tiring way, and it is often a non-appreciative way, but nonetheless it is still a way to make a living.

A 9 to 5 job is the typical way and place where most Americans spend their day. A job that is more than likely thankless and tough. A place where dreams are not admonished and a time clock is the great chief. In other words, your personal goals are not the cornerstone of success, but your ability to follow instructions and keep your work pace is crucial.

Some people are so conformed to their jobs that they fear doing anything else.

Most Americans are conditioned to work for other people the majority of their lives. Some folks would not have it any other way, they live to serve others. It is okay, if that is what you really desire. Sadly, most folks do not know any other way to survive. But, when you know better, you're supposed to do better, right? I believe so. Confidence is the ticket to challenge and eventually conquer any endeavor. Fear is merely pre-conceived failure.

Punching in and punching out, signing in and signing out, what a drag, but someone has to do it. "What a way to make a living, barely getting by, all taking and no giving." Again, Dolly Parton sure said a mouth full that speaks mountains of truisms in today's work force. But let's be honest here, the norm is actually 8 to 5, because the employer wants you to burn your own hour for lunch. You get nothing for free, absolutely nothing.

Of course, people have to make a living, but they should not have to make a living at their own expense. Health and time cannot be replaced but there are two options to wealth. The two ways to have wealth are either you inherit it or you work smart to earn it. It is safe to say that you won't acquire real wealth by working an 8 to 5 job. There are some exceptions to the rule, but for the most part the few folks that gain wealth by working 8 to 5 don't draw much light on the financial radar. Most people who work from 8 to 5 are the nuts and bolts to an engine that makes a system function. For instance, government, state, city, and federal jobs are all a part of a large system that takes multitudes of people to make them function. The majority of people employed by the above- mentioned systems work 8 to 5 and they are a part of the public sector.

Next, there is the private job sector. These systems employ a large number of people as well. Many individuals in these particular jobs work 8 to 5 as well.

One of the interesting things about the private job sector is that they often immolate a pyramid in terms of position and pay structure. Don't be shocked, it's actually true if you take a look at a typical American Corporation. The person at the tiptop is the President/CEO and, undoubtedly, the top moneymaker. The next level would encompass a few high-salaried Sr. Vice Presidents followed by a number of regular Vice Presidents on the next level, who make a decent salary as well. As you move down the pyramid, we find an even wider level, which houses managers and supervisors, who are basic 8 to 5 people too, with just a title. And of course, the bottom level is filled with a bunch of 8 to 5 employees who make substantially less than the folks closer to the top of the pyramid.

It is amazing that people settle for less concerning their families and their own well-being. You and your family deserve better, and just because you are not the president of the company doesn't mean you can't give your family the best. You do not have to live in a mansion but you can own a decent home, your kids do not have to attend private school, but you can provide them with a good education. All adults, especially men, have a responsibility to ensure their family's financial future.

Public Service Employees

Public service employees are the public servants of society. I won't mention who they are, because you know who they are. They are good people who do a necessary job. Their jobs definitely fit the criteria of being bonafide careers. Oftentimes, these types of careers are sought after by many people in society due to their alleged job security. Yes, job security. People love to boast about job security from a career that will never allow them to excel pass a certain financial stature. It's a good way to make a living, but will you thwart the possibilities of new financial heights after retirement. Most public servants will live at their limit-level, meaning they will most likely never live beyond the financial salaries that they accepted with their public service position.

Nonetheless, some folks are absolutely fine with living at their limit-level. This is simply good advice to have a back-up plan in place for possible unforeseen circumstances.

Hard Work

Hard work is exactly what it is, hard work. Unfortunately, hard work is no guarantee for success. If hard work was a guarantee for success, there would be tons of 8 to 5, hardworking Americans acquiring tons of wealth. On the contrary, most hardworking Americans are contributing to someone else's wealth. But, if you are working hard within your own business arena to build wealth for your own family's future, then yes, keep up the hard work.

Loyalty

Loyalty is a rare commodity, which is not necessarily exhibited, or reciprocated by your employer. Most employers feel they owe you nothing for your perfect attendance record and your great on-time record. Your mere presence in their facility or job site is reward enough. In other words, you are lucky to have a job according to your employer. Undoubtedly, loyalty is not a two-way street.

Dedication

Dedication is great and it is desirable in the workplace. For every slouch in the workplace, there are several employees who are very dedicated and willing to give their all each and every day when they go to work. Dedication is a good thing, but it doesn't ensure a job promotion. If you are one of the lucky ones to receive a job promotion, just pray that your 8 to 5 job doesn't suddenly turn into an 8 to 7 nightmare, just for a little more money. You may be asked to be away from your family longer than you desire to be. Our families should be our number one priority.

Stress

On-the-job problems can cause headaches and a magnitude of stress. Stress is dangerous and can affect your health tremendously. Jobs are supposed to provide a way to sustain life and not create stressful situations that can cause serious health problems. Sometimes, 8 to 5 is just not the way to make a living when it is negatively affecting your life. It is not worth your while to jeopardize your well-being due to the confines of a job.

Financial Stability

Financial stability is something that we all should desire for our families. The question is; "Can financial stability actually be secured by working 8 to 5?" Financial stability is very hard to achieve, but it can be accomplished through shrewd investments, disciplined savings methods, and ultimately a backup-plan (B,C,D, & E) to support your 8 to 5 plan 'A'. If you are working for someone, your employer would be considered your plan 'A'. If you develop your own source of income on a full-time basis, that would be considered your plan 'A'.

It is essential for your financial future to have a back-up plan if an 8 to 5 job is your only source of income. A back-up plan is an absolute must. Your family deserves to be financially protected during unforeseen circumstances. As you know, anything can happen at any moment in life to change the financial road that you are currently traveling on.

The necessities of a back-up plan and financial security for your family will be covered in a latter chapter.

Lay-offs

What if you get laid-off from your 8 to 5 job, or the company goes out of business, what are you going to do? Many companies downsize and some others outsource their manpower to other countries. It happens each and everyday across America, people lose jobs and they don't have any type of security blanket to keep themselves and their families afloat. These situations are downright hurtful, but shameful, in the sense that a simple plan 'B' could have helped to keep their financial boat afloat.

This chapter is not meant to be a knock-out punch to folks that work an 8 to 5 job, it is simply meant to be a wake-up call. As you progress in life, your personal needs will often change, but more times than not, that 8 to 5 job will remain the same until the dead-end sign appears. Just as a winding road often conceals its contents, so it is as that dead-end sign appears when you least expect. You deserve better, so give your life light at the end of the tunnel.

Benefits and Pension

The one thing that is most important to individuals, when first seeking a job or career, is the type of benefits being offered by the employer. Benefits are usually a great selling point. If benefits are in place, it must be a great job, most folks believe.

And, it is true, benefits are very important to have when you're married and have children. But, the reality is, you are literally becoming dependent on your employer to a certain extent. If the company goes out of business, or if you are fired, etc., your family will have no healthcare or dental coverage. That is why it is important to have a subsequent plan in place. You should always want to be in control of your family's well-being, instead of letting someone else be in control.

A pension is the sum of money paid out to you from your employer, following your retirement. The amount of money you receive will most likely be a set amount of funds, and it probably will not provide you with financial freedom. Unfortunately, many individuals have to take on new employment following retirement, just to make ends meet. As stated earlier, a subsequent plan could possibly keep you in control of your future instead of your employer. Retirement should be the time that you actually retire, and not the time that you begin to make a living.

Retirement

Let's face the facts, there are a few employers that provide a **great** retirement package. There are a number of employers that provide a **good** retirement package and there are even more employers that offer a very **menial** retirement plan to their 8 to 5 employees. As reality races to full effect, and retirement time has come, you quickly realize that retirement is not actually retirement. Your departure from your job is just a break in the action and you must secure additional employment to survive. The joyous retirement years that you dreamed about are suddenly times when you struggle to make ends meet and you can't enjoy the pleasures of life as you should. You have given an employer 25 to 30 years of your life and you can't even stay home with your family or travel to see the world. But, you did get a company watch that isn't even real gold. These are the sad realities of our current times.

I urge you to have a back-up plan for you and your family. It is truly the only way to go.

I'm just a common man with a simple plan.

3

Education

As children, many of our parents harped on the subject of education. From sun up to sun down, we had to hear the speech of how education was an absolute must. Education was said to be the lifeline and guarantee that our lives would be good. We were told that more than likely we would land a good job and we would be able to have food, a home and clothing. Without an education we were told that the future would be grim and success would be an impossible task. Some of you can relate to these sentiments and some of you may have experienced totally different speeches concerning education from your parents. Nonetheless, I would think that it is safe to say that in the majority of households in America, education is thought to be a very important commodity to possess. Education is a subject matter that was kept in the forefront of most of our minds while growing up.

Our educational system is broken down into several levels and each level is meant to develop our minds appropriately. Some people began their educational process in pre-school and worked their way through to the 6th grade.

Next, there is middle school. Then there is the exciting experience of high school.

Upon leaving high school, the stakes of life change, according to what is mentioned in the proceeding paragraphs.

Before I continue to speak on the subject of education, I must interject the fact that many successful business people didn't attend college and are now living the American Dream. There are some high school graduates that are making the type of living that we were taught only applied to the college graduate. *There are many individuals in America that are very wealthy and education was not their ticket.*

Many of our parents told us that if we didn't attend college, we had to immediately obtain a job. They also warned, in no uncertain terms, that residency was not guaranteed unless attending college was part of the plan. Most of our parents welcomed our presence at home or even offered to pay our college tuition and our dorm housing or off-ground housing as long as we attended college. After God and family, education was like a very good friend, you just had to have it.

Just think about it, countless college graduates leave school with high hopes and dreams of immediately joining the workforce, and many are likely to be disappointed. Where is the logic in attending college if you don't get the opportunity to practice what you've learned within the institutions of higher education? And what about the parents who've gone out on the limb by spending thousands of dollars for their son or daughter's education and learn they can't even get a job. But, as it is clearly known in America, if you don't have that piece of paper (degree) no interview and certainly no job will be offered. There are even many students who obtain a college education and never utilize the particular field of study that they chose while in college.

With certain fields of study, there are certainly professional organizations in society that will provide a great financial award to individuals after receiving their college degree. The real order of the day is that a college degree cannot guarantee financial freedom. Of course there are exceptions to any rule. For example, individuals in pursuit of becoming a doctor, will spend several years in medical school. They will also spend years completing a residency program at a medical facility to assist them in mastering their craft. These individuals should make a very good salary after they become board certified physicians.

A college education is a great asset to possess, but coupled with basic business skills and a dose of common sense, no one should be able to stop you from achieving your goals?

Parents should want their children to achieve the highest level of education possible, that's normal. There is no doubt that education is a valuable asset, and more than likely your level of education will dictate the type of position you land in the job market. It is unfortunate that there are no guarantees of immediate employment after graduating from college. Just make sure you equip yourself to compete properly in the job market.

If you are one of those students in limbo between school and the job market, take the opportunity to learn everything you can about basic business and begin to learn the importance of protecting your financial future. Learn to be a savvy financial investor. Create avenues to support yourself so that you will not have to rely on others for your success. Come up with ideas and strategies for at least a plan B and a plan C. These two plans will be your future support system to your plan A. With this type of thought process operating within you, it is now time for you to make a living. You are now prepared to initiate your plan A, which is the start of your career.

Once you initiate your plan 'A', hopefully, it will be within an established firm and field you are passionate about pursuing. Learn as much as possible about the business practices of your field as you slowly lay the groundwork for self-employment.

I'm just a common man with a simple plan.

4

I Think I Want To Be Rich

How many times have you heard people say that they want to be rich? Are they really being honest with themselves? To become rich is serious stuff. To become rich is not for chumps. Most people have no clue about what it takes to become rich. If you think it's so easy, then why aren't the majority of people you know rich? I'll tell you why, because it takes a lot of work to be rich. Most people don't have the work ethic that it takes to be rich. There are some rules to becoming rich and I will just name a few.

You must be focused. When you are focused that means your aim is set directly on the prize. If your prize is to be rich, never change your aim.

You must work smart. There is no substitute for smart work. Smart workers usually obtain their goals within a certain period of time. They simply plan and then proceed.

Develop a viable plan and implement that plan with prudence. You must have a plan in place before you proceed towards your goal to be rich.

You must possess good work habits. Good work habits will more than likely lead you to success. Remain disciplined in the pruning of your craft.

Conduct your research. Don't attempt to go into any venture with blinders on. You must have data that supports the process of your venture. Don't spend too much time on the analysis, because oftentimes that will lead to paralysis and you get nowhere. If the investment or business project is good, jump in before the opportunity is lost.

Think positive at all times. A positive attitude is a soothing sedative as you move in pursuit of your goal to be rich.

Don't allow negative people to thwart your future dreams to be rich. Most negative people have no vision, so they want to throw poisonous darts at your dreams. Their whole job is to spout off negative comments and attempt to destroy your destiny, because they have no worthwhile plans for their own life.

Patience is a virtue. You must have patience on your road to becoming rich. If you are expecting a get rich quick, overnight project, you'd be better off buying lottery tickets seven days a week in every state in America and chances are, you still won't get rich. Patience is key on the road to success. Take your time and nurture your business as you grow towards becoming rich. Most people want microwave money, better known as a quick fix to their financial woes.

Listen to the experts who are affiliated with the craft that you have chosen for success. There is no substitute for seeking advice from the experts who have gone before you in business. It makes perfect sense to learn from individuals who have already become rich in the venture that you have chosen to become successful in.

Read as many books pertaining to your craft as you possibly can. There is no substitute for knowledge.

And finally, don't do what the majority of people do once they think they want to be rich and the road gets a little bumpy, "**Don't Quit**!" Quitters absolutely, positively cannot be rich. They do not have the ability to put their hearts and minds into their business venture. They pretend for a brief moment that they want success, but inwardly they really have no means or purpose to complete their alleged business venture. They go through the motions and even pretend to demonstrate the elements of a person who is pursuing the road of success, but inwardly, they really don't have what it takes to join the club of the rich and famous.

There are countless individuals, who have produced products or started businesses, that actually quit before coming out of the starting blocks. Why waste your time even starting a business or producing a product if you are going to quit within a short period of time. Make it easy on yourself and don't waste your time starting the process.

My advice to you is simply admit the truth to yourself, you don't want to be rich. The truth of the matter is, most people think they want to be rich but; unfortunately, they don't have what it takes to hit the mark. It is not meant for everyone to be rich, so, if that is you, accept reality and move on. But, if you are one of the rare individuals that can accept the challenge to be rich, it's time to get to work.

I'm just a common man with a simple plan.

5

Common Sense Makes Business Cents

In one of the previous chapters, the focus was on education and its benefits in the workplace. There really is truth in the statement that someone can be an educated fool. Some of them are the very people that won't hire your son or daughter after they have graduated from college. Truth be told, all the degrees in the world cannot replace the need for common sense. Why would a person bother gaining a college education and not utilize it correctly? Why would a person be employed and not understand all aspects of the company, as well as the type of benefit package and pay? Common sense can't be bought nor can it be transplanted, but thankfully it can be passed on if a person is able to absorb it. Possessing common sense is a must in today's business world. Common sense will carry you and protect you when nothing else will. Common sense is the safety and security that protects you from being misguided into bad business decisions. Common sense is the sixth sense that embodies an individual's mind and body and allows him or her to respond to situations in the proper manner.

Unfortunately, common sense is not too common in the workplace. Oftentimes, people really don't know what is best for themselves and their families. People do not understand the advantages of being mentally prepared to stand up for themselves and make the proper business decisions when necessary.

It is very sad that many folks are so dependent on others for every little thing. Individuals go through their whole careers without understanding their own personal business and have no clue of basic finances.

Please educate yourselves regarding your personal finances, learn the value of saving money, research various investments, diversify when you do invest, and investigate the advantages of acquiring some kind of home-based business.

The combination of a college education and common sense is a powerful combination.

Business-Minded Business

Many people are proud to state the fact that they are business-minded. What is business-minded? I imagine it means that you have a mind for business. What is a mind for business? I imagine it means that you can take care of the business at hand. What is the business at hand? I imagine it is your current business that you are handling. My point is that we don't always mean what we say when it comes to business dealings. We mean well, but some of us really don't have the tools to be business-minded. For example, if you were fortunate to buy a popular franchise, you would most likely have to attend company training, and you would probably receive a company packet with important information pertaining to the franchise. You will receive the necessary tools to become business savvy as well as business-minded regarding your franchise.

For those of you who are contemplating going into a business venture, I encourage you to prepare yourself to become business-minded. Preparation can be done by researching the company or the kind of business that you are thinking about exploring. There are books, seminars, or you may want to make direct contact with the very folks who are in the type of business that you are seeking to enter.

Preparation in business is a definite necessity if you are serious about opening a business.

I urge you not to go into business just because you desire to feel business-minded. And, please don't pay any money for a business whether it is six hundred dollars or six million dollars without conducting proper due diligence.

Make A Living

Life is much too short not to enjoy it to the fullest. People are so busy trying to make a living that they forget to live. Living is enjoying the great things that life has to offer. Moreover, the greatest feeling is to enjoy life with the ones you love. Some people work themselves to death literally, without ever having the opportunity to live and have fun.

The best reward in life is to be able to dictate the manner in which your time is spent.

A workaholic's reward is simply more work. Workaholics can't stop and take the time to realize that they really need to make a living. A workaholic needs to learn how to make a living and not let a living make them.

Going to work, and simply doing a job, and returning home is not living. That is work by every definition of the word.

Making good financial decisions on behalf of your family and yourself is great. That's the way it should be. On the other hand, those decisions should be administered with prudent judgment.

Have Fun

Take some time to have some fun. Weekend excursions are simply teasers, you need to take long vacations, so that you can really enjoy the company of your family. Go to the movies more often and enjoy a good flick together. Go out together to the ballgame and root on your favorite team. Better yet, relax on the bank of a beautiful lake, and cast out your fishing rods together.

There is nothing comparable to spending quality time with your loved-ones. I don't believe that people dream to work and be apart from their families. Real living is being able to share, appreciate, and spend time with the folks you love the most on the entire earth. Now that's good living. Take a chill pill and have some real fun. Enjoy the blessings that God has placed before you.

I'm just a common man with a simple plan.

6

Believe To Achieve

You must first believe before you can achieve anything in life. Every man, woman, boy and girl encompasses an inner-gauge that measures his or her faith and endurance. The more faith you have the more you endure. The less faith you have the less you endure. The bible says in Philippians 4:13 ? *"I can do all things through Christ who strengthens me."* Such a powerful bible verse with life-changing possibilities.

It literally pays, to put your faith into practice.

Keep The Faith

Believe and never doubt your abilities. It all starts with you. Your faith can move mountains if you literally believe in your efforts. No one can hamper you from achieving your goals but you. With God before you, who can be against you? I urge you to put God first before you take on any endeavor. He will never fail you. You can only fail yourself.

Eagles vs. Crows

Birds are very interesting species. Some of their behavior can be compared to human beings. Eagles are beautiful birds of prey that have the ability to soar far above the land. They are strong and their vision is excellent. It is documented that eagles have the ability to fly at altitudes equal to that of jet airplanes. Eagles are such awesome birds.

Next, there are the crows, a bird that does not have the ability to soar far above the land. Matter of fact, crows hang out closer to the earth, looking for scraps of food, and they pester other birds when given the opportunity. The eagle is the superior bird between the two, but the crow still chooses to pester the eagle whenever possible. Instead of challenging the crow, the far superior eagle chooses to simply soar to a higher altitude that crows have no ability to accomplish. Eagles simply go about their business and forfeit the hassle of dealing with crows. We as humans should imitate the behavior of eagles when faced with adversity or negative counterparts. It is better to rise to a higher frame of mind and go about your business. Do not allow negative people to hamper any opportunity that you wish to pursue.

Integrity

Integrity is the ability to exhibit honesty and trustworthy traits. You will go a very long way in life by being a man or woman of integrity. Never allow any amount of money to thwart your relationships with people. The love of money, not money, is the root to most evil.

No Excuses

In life, we must be responsible for our actions whether positive or negative. You should not make any excuses for the decisions you make in life. There are good consequences when we make good decisions and there are bad consequences when we make bad decisions. Whether it is in business or life in general, a decision is a choice that you make as an individual. We do have to live with the decisions we make in life.

Satisfied Being Satisfied

Are you satisfied being satisfied? It does not cost you any effort to be satisfied in your current state of affairs. Most people are satisfied with their situation, whether they wish to admit it or not. Most people are satisfied with their jobs, their homes, their limited leisure activities, their financial status and their lack of time freedom. Are most people really satisfied being satisfied, or is it true that most people are just too lazy to make a change in their life? Some people would rather settle for less than to exert a bit of energy to elevate their current situation. Why would a person accept less for themselves or their family members? There are always opportunities to improve upon your current situation if you simply make an effort. If you choose to settle for less and simply be satisfied with your current situation, you leave the door of opportunity wide open for the next person to take advantage of improving their life.

Satisfied being satisfied can possibly stunt your physical health, your mental growth, and your economic situation. You owe it to yourself and family members to go beyond being satisfied. Challenge yourself to explore the blessings that are in your path. Taking advantage of an opportunity can possibly change your life forever.

Be the best that you can be at whatever you chose to do. Never, ever be satisfied with the minimum of your total potential.

I Don't Have Time

How many times, if ever, have you said, "I don't have time?" I know exactly why you don't have time. The answer is simple, "Time has you." When you are hampered by time, there is not much you can do. When you have no time, you are what is referred to as time-broke. When you are time- broke, the goodness and good things of life suffer, such as, spending quality time with your family and friends.

We often find time to do the things that we really desire to do, even though they may not be conducive to our well-being or future success.

The key to having more time for you and your loved-ones is to do more in terms of securing your finances. By controlling the avenues in which your finances are disbursed, you will begin to control your total time outlook. As you control more of your time, you will have the opportunity to enjoy the things you cherish most in life.

Chance introduces change and change brings about opportunity. You have to allow yourself time to be able to pursue opportunities that are presented to you. The right opportunity can bring about a significant amount of wealth, which usually provides you the time to cater to yourself. In essence, you will be time-rich instead of being time- broke.

Time is so valuable. We must utilize it in a sufficient manner. For once in your life, make sure that time is on your side.

Invest In You

You hold the key to unlocking your own personal journey to success. Don't crack open the door, open it wide and seek life's benefits so that you will find them.

By investing in yourself, you are taking full responsibility for laying the groundwork for your future. People may disappoint you and lie to you, but only you can fail yourself. God has not given you the spirit of fear. You were created by an awesome God that knows you better than you know yourself. God did not give another person the ability to believe in him or herself more than He has given you the capability of believing in yourself. You do have the equipment and the ability necessary to do great things. You must simply expose your faith. Faith is your most powerful tool.

You are truly the navigator of your destiny but you must grab hold of the steering wheel of life, proceed forward, and never look in the rearview mirror.

Do not simply survive, but strive to be the best you can be through all economic times.

Dream A Little Dream

Dreams are truly for dreamers. If you don't dream, you have literally deprived your imagination of being a light beam for your future. Just think if you could do whatever you wanted to do whenever you wanted to on any day of the week. Imagine if you could buy anything you wanted anytime you felt like it. How would it be not to have to punch a time clock or hear your supervisor yell at you for unnecessary reasons? Imagine being able to travel across the world on a whim. Picture living in the home of your dream with all the state-of-the art amenities. Think about how it would feel to have your children's children financially secure for the rest of their lives. It sounds crazy, right? All endeavors start with a dream, which is simply a modified thought. Combine your thoughts, with the strength of your inner spirit, coupled with a bit of faith and you can accomplish the world.

Take on the World

I implore you and I challenge you to go take on the world, and be the best you can be at whatever occupation or personal business you decide to do in life. Life should be fun and you should prosper as you make a living.

I'm just a common man with a simple plan.

7

The Internet and Home-based Businesses

We are living in an era where new technology is developed almost daily. There seems to be so many possibilities, right at our fingertips, if we would just extend our hand to grasp them. Today, the world does provide a number of opportunities to individuals, it is simply their duty to seek them.

In chapter two, I spoke in detail regarding the typical American that works the basic 8 to 5 job. I have always believed that if you must continue in your 8 to 5 job, at least have some type of back-up plan to support you in case of an emergency; such as, a job lay-off or an unfortunate injury.

The internet is certainly not new, but it is still the most ingenious tool in modern time. Of course, that is my opinion, but I'm sure many people will agree. The internet helps to deliver the world to your doorstep, by way of the world-wide-web. How amazing to have a vehicle that connects the world in a matter of seconds. The depth of information available on the internet is enormous and growing every day. Government agencies, Corporate America, newsgathering organizations, universities (both large and small) and many other types of companies can be accessed through the internet. These same organizations and companies utilize the internet for their own internal operations. In fact, most businesses conduct their operations through the utilization of the internet.

What better method could there be to communicate globally, than with the internet? The internet is a unique information source. I believe that the wave of the future will be channeled directly through the utilization of the internet. There is no explanation needed to exemplify the success that is evident by way of the use of the internet.

Google, AOL and Yahoo are some of the largest internet companies in the world and they are surely multi-billion dollar companies that have experienced proven success.

The number of products that are sold over the internet is too numerous to list. We are now in a world of "click and order." Again, the internet is by no means new technology, but it is a necessary means that works. The saying goes, "If it ain't broke, don't fix it."

A Home-Based Business

Have you ever dreamed of being in business for yourself? What better way to utilize the internet than with the operation of a home-based business. You are in business and operating from the comfort of your home. Several individuals have created their home-based business by embracing the fantastic world of the internet.

Imagine new business ideas being turned into enormous
realities simply because of the onslaught of the internet.
It is amazing that a small business can be introduced to
the world in a matter of seconds. While home-based
businesses may have been unpopular in the recent past,
they are certainly the wave of the future in today's households.

Marketing and Advertising

Several companies choose to promote their products via the internet. It is a brilliant vehicle to reach the
masses of people across the entire world. The world
would seem one-dimensional if it were not for the presence of the internet. We can practically purchase anything in the world from the internet. Just think of the
many product ads that pop up when you are viewing
your favorite website. Many companies understand the
importance of individuals viewing various websites, so
they take the initiative to place advertisements in hopes
that sales of their particular product can be generated.

The Possibilities

There are several companies that have become very
wealthy due to their utilization of the internet. One company that comes to mind is Google. The Google company has captured a great market by way of the internet.
Google is doing extremely well and their growth appears
to be endless. One share of Google's stock is worth several hundred dollars. You too can take hold of the possibilities that life has to offer. I urge you to put on your
business cap and climb the mountain. There is room at
the top, but you can't stop.

The Communicator

The majority of people utilize the internet as a common source to communicate with one another on a daily basis worldwide. The internet is more preferred for communication than the average home telephone. As a matter of fact, people spend hours at a time on the internet, researching their favorite topic, or simply surfing the web to find out the latest happenings. The internet is definitely a tremendous resource for information as well as a brilliant link to connect the world.

Several Advantages

There are a number advantages regarding the ownership of a home-based business. First of all, there is the convenience of being at home operating your own business. You are your own boss, so I guess that means you tell yourself when to take lunches and breaks. Moreover, you establish your hours of operation. I guess that makes you totally in control of your own situation. Secondly, there are several tax deductions associated with home-based businesses. Huge tax deductions can equal big money. You would be surprised at the various items you can write off due to owning your home-based business. Why not take advantage of an opportunity to retain your money. It is advisable that you consult with a tax specialist so that you can take full advantage of the numerous tax incentives that you may qualify for as a home-based business owner.

The Fantastic Gadget

The fantastic gadget that is most often utilized to channel the life-stream of the internet is the computer. The desktop and laptop are the most popular styles of computers that are utilized across the entire world to distribute information. This unique machine is the heartbeat that pumps words, pictures and sound through a multi-network of billions of internet avenues. Computers have changed the way the world does business as well as the way that people communicate with one another. Many households in America do contain a computer. Also, the majority of businesses across America have computers behind their doors as well.

There is no reason to delay, because you have the tools to start your business today.

I'm just a common man with a simple plan.

8

Plan Your Future

I believe that each of us as Americans must plan for the future. There are no guarantees in life, but having a plan can help keep your direction in focus. What is life worth without a solid plan? There is an old cliché that is often quoted stating that, " People fail to plan, they don't plan to fail." However, more often than not many people do fail in life because they fail to plan. A plan is merely a formulation of an idea that is put into action. So, many people have big ideas to do great things, but they never take the initiative to implement their plan. No one should be without a plan and no one should put their plans on hold. There is no time like the present to move forward with your goals. Only you have the power to cease the implementation of your plan.

Just Do It

Nike Inc., created a slogan of a few words, but its meaning speaks volumes to those who apply the simple phrase, "Just Do It." Oh, how I agree with Nike, Inc. I attempt to follow that motto with everything that I need to do. When you take the initiative to do things without hesitation, more than likely, you will complete your task.

Excuses are a dime a dozen and many people would rather make excuses instead of making plans for their future. Excuses and success are allergic to one another, they just don't mix. You cannot implement a legitimate plan and then make excuses to keep from moving forward. Excuses are merely your own personal ticket to forfeit your ideas and to thwart your dreams. I urge you to formulate your plans no matter how great or minor they may be and, yes, "Just Do It."

Plan A, B, C…

Most of us have heard that we should have a back-up plan in life. Some adhere to that advice and some don't. So many people are so satisfied and comfortable with their plan 'A' that they don't even bother to seek additional plans for their life. Our primary jobs tend to be our plan 'A'. No matter how much security you think you have with your plan 'A', I urge you to still seek additional plans for your life. What if your plan 'A' ceases to exist for unknown reasons, what would you do? Would you be able to pay your mortgage? How about your car note, would you be able to pay it? What about your utilities, can you keep them up and running? No matter how remote you think the chances are that you may lose your plan 'A', statistics show that it can happen when you least expect. Or, as stated in an earlier chapter, you could possibly have your pension or retirement pay substantially reduced. Would you be able to sustain your family's lifestyle if this were to happen to you? No one should take a chance by jeopardizing their future with a lack of finances. There is no better plan, than a subsequent plan, that protects your total plan.

What is a plan 'B'? An adequate plan 'B' should be able to sustain your plan 'A' if it were to be altered or temporarily removed. An excellent plan 'B' can totally substitute for a plan 'A' that is no longer in existence. Of course, this would be the ideal situation if someone were to lose his or her primary job (plan 'A') or their pension or retirement pay. An example of a plan 'B' would be owning your own business.

What is the purpose of a plan 'C'? A good plan 'C' can support a plan 'A' and/or a plan 'B'. A plan 'C' is not meant to sustain you solely on its own, but it would definitely be a good source of income. An example of a plan 'C' would be various investments; such as, owning percentages in a company; whereby you are able to generate a stable income and you have access to the earned revenue. That would be a good financial support system. What is the purpose of a good plan 'D' and 'E'? Plan 'D' and 'E' can support your plan 'C' if you are experiencing problems with plan 'A' and 'B'.

Your plan 'D' and 'E' can consist of income-bearing assets; such as, real estate. A combination of several rental properties can generate great income. Additional options for back-up plans can be in the form of mutual funds, stocks, bonds, and money market accounts. If you were savvy enough to have several plans in place, and your plan 'A' has failed for whatever reason, it is likely that you will recover quickly. People who plan properly rarely experience total failure. They simply adjust their finances and move on with their lives. The key is to be prepared for whatever situation life may unexpectedly throw your way.

Investments

Responsible people desire to have their money grow in the future by way of investments. There are numerous avenues in which to invest your money, but you must conduct the research to find out what is best for you. A future financial return on your invested money is the ultimate goal. A seasoned investor looks for good opportunities. Good opportunities usually equal good investments. The best way to ensure your future as a good investor is to educate yourself and seek advice from experts.

Your family's future is worth your time to do the necessary research to ensure financial security. When you invest, do it wisely.

Credit…Credit…Credit

How often do we hear financial folks talk about the importance of good credit? Comedians often make brilliant jokes about many folks having bad credit. But, lets face reality, credit is crucial in this day and age.

I remember growing up as a kid when my parents used to take my siblings and I to Disneyland. Back in the day, when you entered Disneyland, you would have to purchase tickets for rides separately from the entry fee. The most coveted ticket was the 'E' ticket. This particular ticket allowed you access to the best rides at Disneyland. The 'E' ticket was definitely the ticket to possess if you wanted the most fun.

The point I'm trying to make is that good credit is like an 'E' ticket used to be at Disneyland, it's a good thing. Good credit is your ticket to many great opportunities in society. Your good credit rating should be maintained and not misused. Good credit is not a valid reason to make undue purchases or to max-out your credit cards.

Good credit can be a slight curse if you do not manage it properly. According to many credit experts, there are certain practices that can be followed to prevent your good credit score from being affected. For example, if you pay off a high credit card bill, don't close the account, leave it open. Credit reporting agencies will give you favorable scores when you have available credit. Ironically, maintaining 20% of your available credit leaves a credit history that can be tracked by credit bureaus. If you have all zero balances, the credit bureaus have nothing to rate you on. Moreover, numerous credit inquiries may cause you to appear unstable and these practices can surely diminish your credit score. Lastly, financed credit is not as good as a company tells you it is. You are simply delaying the payment on something that you want now. Credit reporting agencies view "no payment now" offers as a risk and will possibly lower your credit rating. Even if you make your payments on time, "no payment and no interest" is not a good practice.

In addition, for those of you who are interested in the mystique of the purpose of Fico scores, I will spell it out to you as simple as I can.

Fico scores are the probability rating of the likelihood that you will have a 30-day late payment within the next 12 months. This is the golden rule that credit bureaus abide by.

Unfortunately, if you do not have good credit, your access to housing, business loans and other financial opportunities can be severely hampered. Good credit is essential in a society that is driven by one's Fico scores.

Borderline Criminal

This small segment of information is mainly for men. There are certain things that men just have to do for their families to be the leader, which they are called by God to be. A man should protect as well as provide for his family at all cost. There is no taller calling than for a man to provide security for his spouse and children. A man that does not provide for his family, or help to secure future finances for his children, should be ashamed of himself. It is borderline criminal not to take the time to leave some type of financial legacy for your family. What is the purpose of living if your legacy is simply your death? Do something great for yourself now that will ultimately be passed on as a blessing for your children's lives later. You can start by obtaining an adequate life insurance plan.

Personal Experience

There is nothing like hearing something from the horse's mouth as they say. I am also a firm believer in the notion that you must practice what you preach. I truly believe that having multiple plans to support your plan 'A' is a must. I also work a regular job, but my wife and I have made a concerted effort to obtain multiple back-up plans to support my plan 'A', which is my regular job. Without delving into deep detail regarding our subsequent plans, I will just state them in general. This is in no way to brag or boast, but to simply state that when others provide you with good financial information, listen and apply the information. I give God the glory for the things he has done. We have truly been covered with the FOG (Favor of God). At one time, I felt guilty for being tremendously blessed, which is crazy. Pastor Joel Osteen, said it best, "Don't apologize for God's goodness."

First of all, we live in a home that we never imagined buying based upon one salary. Now, we own several homes throughout the United States. I believe real estate is still a great investment. We have several money market and certificate accounts, and we allow the interest to compound, which is good financial savvy, I was told. We also own stock in several companies. When our stock is high we sell, when it is low we buy more. Next, as partners, we own percentages in a popular fast food chain. People love to eat, so I guess it is a good investment. We also own an entertainment company in reference to television, film and my published books. It makes a multitude of sense to invest in my own endeavors. It is good business sense to embrace what you love to do. Oprah did it. She embraced her talent, marketed herself, and look what happened. The rest is history. And last, but not least, my wife and I purchased a travel agency. What is so unique about the business is that it is a home-based business and it is on the world-wide-web, the internet. That's right, we own an on-line travel agency. Out of all the businesses we own, this one was the least expensive, yet, the return on investment has been awesome. I tell close friends, and even people I meet, that they do not have to invest large sums of money to have a great business. Our online travel business was purchased for under $500.00, which is a far cry from the thousands of dollars we have spent on our other investments. As you can clearly see from the above summary, we have a plan A,B,C,D,E and beyond. Your future can be bright if you help create the light. We are not multi-millionaires; but, one day soon, we will be. God has truly been good to us spiritually and financially. This is my favorite bible scripture that I love to quote, "I can do all things through Christ who strengthens me." *Phil. 4:13*

I'm just a common man with a simple plan.

9

Networking and Marketing

Networking and marketing equals network marketing. Some business people cringe when they hear the words network marketing. Undoubtedly, these people have no clue that marketing and networking are the most credible way to do business. Marketing entails selling and promoting, while networking is the exchange of information and services. *A friend by the name of **Calvin Ellerbe**, **YTB Director**, said it best, "Networking is not net-wishing or net-waiting, networking means actually working towards a common goal."*

The process of combining marketing and networking is necessary to build relationships within the business world, which will ultimately help to grow your business.

Do not undermine your current network marketing business by attempting to offer subsequent networking opportunities to others. You will appear unstable and fickle to potential clients and your credibility will be diminished. You do not want financial conflict; you should strive for financial cohesiveness. You must display a true concerted effort to work your initial business and first believe in your product so others can believe in you.

Once your efforts have afforded you the benefits of network marketing, you will soon experience relationship marketing. As your relationships continue to grow, your business is bound to flourish beyond your wildest dreams.

Multiple Streams of Income

Having multi-streams of income is definitely a great financial goal to shoot for. Money being generated from different avenues equals multi-streams of income. Multi-streams of opportunities are not necessarily equivalent to multi-streams of income. You must generate income from each opportunity source to produce multi-streams of income.

For example, you may have income being generated from rental property, you may have income from high-interest bearing money market accounts and CD's, you may have income being generated from long-term asset investments, you may have income being generated from a traditional business operation; and finally, you may have income being generated from your current network marketing business. The more avenues of income you generate, the more wealth you will create for you and your family.

Assets...Liabilities...Expenses

As I stated in the beginning of the this book, I am not a financial wizard, but I do understand the concept of basic business. I do realize that we all have expenses and some of us have more than others. I also realize that poor people are usually engulfed by expenses as they try their best to survive the pounding of life in any way they can. Rich people have expenses as well, but those costs have little affect on their lives, because they thrive off their assets. On the other hand, the majority of the middle-class are known to wallow in the arena of liabilities as they rely on their work wages to sustain their lifestyle.

It is no secret that having assets is what we all should shoot for to bring real financial security to our lives. The key is to have income-generating assets. As you begin to secure income-generating assets, you will soon have streams of money that will surpass your liabilities. I would imagine that the more assets you have, the more wealth you gain, which may very well result in you becoming rich.

If you are a member of the middle-class, do not be fooled about the hype of buying bigger or better just because your linear (wages for work) way of life has increased. A big home, an expensive car and a high credit card limits does not necessarily mean that you have arrived. It actually equates to living on the edge without a parachute. If you are spending the majority of your money on a house, car, and credit card payments and you just have enough money left over to pay your basic living expenses, that is very dangerous living. You have just joined the liabilities club in full force. The problem with this scenario is that if for some reason you become unemployed, your source of income would not exist. Again, I urge you to secure assets and to keep your expenses less than your cash flow. Most middle-class individuals can make an adjustment that can easily put them on the path of investing in income-generating assets.

Rich people have mastered the art of seeking and retaining assets that produce massive amounts of income, which sustain them without having a traditional job.

I truly believe that poor people can make a change from their lives being consumed by the overwhelming flood of expenses. First, seek help from someone that is not expensive, but qualified, to help with advice to get you out of your unfortunate situation. After you proceed to get your expenses to a manageable level, start to save money by paying yourself, every little bit will help. Rich people and the middle-class are not the only ones that can invest in their future. With the onslaught of the internet and home-based businesses, miracles have occurred with individuals who have had very little money. Your goal should always be to have some type of income-generating asset no matter what your status is in life.

Residual Income vs. Linear Income

You do not have to be dependent forever on your linear income, which is work for wages. You can explore the freedom of residual income that provides generational wealth. Residual income is money earned by you, but at a particular point, your initial efforts continuously generate more money in spite of you. Once it starts, it keeps going and going and going and your family benefits from you working smarter, not harder. Linear income equals work for pay. No work, no pay. Which would you prefer, linear income or residual income? Let's just face the facts, most Americans have no idea what residual income is. We are so programmed to exchange our precious time for wages. The problem is that our wages are oftentimes unequal to the precious time that we spend working. Work for wages is a tough cookie to swallow, but it is something that we as Americans have practiced for many years. Some people just love being a robot. Some people just love having their buttons pushed by someone else. Some people just do not have the guts to take their lives into their own hands to extend it to the next level. I am not saying anything contrary from what the big moneymakers are saying, I am simply speaking their language in a slightly different way.

Residual income is the kind of income that you have to experience for yourself to understand that it can truly change your life.

Linear income is something most of you have been experiencing for the majority of your life, so needless to say, I don't have to explain a process to you that you know very well. YTB can provide great residual income. It is up to you to make the change.

I'm just a common man with a simple plan

10

Why—YTB

Disclaimer: My intentions are not to push the YTB Network upon you as a business venture. My wish is only to help you with encouragement about an opportunity that has worked for my wife and I. The main goal is for you to do something, not necessarily YTB, but something as a financial back-up plan for your life.

What is your why in life? Why do you do the things that you do? What is the reason that drives you to want to achieve things in life? Many directors in YTB state, "Your why must make you cry."

I want to take this moment to share an opportunity with you that has literally changed our lives. As I stated in the last chapter, compared to all of the other businesses and investments we own, YTB is truly the diamond in the rough.

You can also purchase your own business. There is no time like the right time, which is now. YTB is a great company that folks are just starting to discover. You are truly in for a ride, no pun intended, when you purchase this awesome, on-line travel business. For starters, I will write about some basic clues that illustrate why YTB is a brilliant company to join forces with for life.

Joy In Business

The biggest joy that we have experienced has been in the sheer happiness of helping others to achieve some of their goals in life. There is nothing like the inner joy you experience when you have helped someone move closer to his/her dreams. My wife and I tell individuals constantly that we are here to assist them anytime they may need us.

You have to be accessible to people that you do business with. People have to know that you have their back through thick and thin and we all know that business can get tough at times. But, don't let discouragement damper your destiny. Success doesn't come in the mode of a single-manned motor boat, but in the cohesive force of cruise ship magnitude. Good people working in sync as a collective force is the key. You should be reliable and you must be trustworthy. Together we succeed and divided we fail.

Financial Freedom

As I eluded to in an earlier chapter, an 8 to 5 job is not likely to be your ticket to financial freedom. There are many advantages to having financial freedom. You must take the initiative to create or discover an opportunity that will allow you to generate unlimited income for yourself. Once you obtain financial freedom, you are financially equipped to support you and your family for several generations to come. You control your time and your time does not control you. The combination of time and money are a great asset.

One of the founders of YTB, J. Lloyd Tomer, better known as "Coach", often speaks of his personal survey that has always scored 100% for him. When he speaks to a group of individuals, whether it be 10 or 100, he poses this question to them, "If you had more time and more money, what would you do more of?" The unanimous choice would be the same each time as individuals stated that they would want to travel. YTB is your travel biz.

Business From Home

What is the most obvious joy of having a home-based business? Yes, you are able to work from home and you have the chance to spend more time with your family. Think about it, no traffic to deal with and the commute is from your bedroom to your home office. You set your own hours and the fun part is you determine how much money you will make based on your own personal efforts.

The tax advantages of owning a home-based business are tremendous. Take a moment to think about the many tools that you might be able to utilize from home to operate your home-based business; for example, your computer, your telephone, your utilities…just to name a few. The best way to know all the deductions that you may be privy to is to consult with a tax expert who is savvy in the home-based business arena. YTB is not the only home-based business on the planet, but it sure is a great one to experience.

A non-stop product

Travel is by far a product that I consider to be non-stop. If travel stops, the world ceases to connect or to function in a productive manner. We are all connected to other cities, states, countries and continents by some form of travel. We travel abundantly for pleasure, we travel strategically for business and we even travel in times of war and pain. Travel is a way of life, because it is constantly a part of our lives. Travel favors no race or gender, because it is truly something that most of us will experience at one time or another. YTB has created a concept that truly links the world together by way of travel.

Some people want a get rich quick product or they desire to embrace a particular product until a new and improved one is developed. The newer product is usually masked by a colorful marketing campaign of the earlier product version. Moreover, YTB makes no false claims of what a product will or won't do. YTB offers the same products that are standard in the travel industry. All the familiar products that your family and friends are accustomed to, are provided by YTB. All your inventory is within the confines of your computer via cyberspace.

False Claims

There is nothing more careless than a company or individual making false claims about a product's value or worth. Such actions are disingenuous and very misleading to a potential consumer.

The great fact about the YTB Travel Network is that the company always delivers its product. If you book a cruise you will get a cruise. If you reserve a rental car, you will receive a car to drive. If you book a plane trip, unless the airline cancels the flight, you will take off. If you order flowers, concert tickets, sporting events or anything else through YTB, you will receive that product.

Integrity In Action

The definition of Integrity in action is "Coach" J. Lloyd Tomer, Scott Tomer and Kim Sorenson, the founders of YTB. They built a company on the principals of honesty, a brilliant product, an excellent marketing concept and professional leadership.

The founders of YTB have mastered the art of combining fun and fortune. They have discovered a business where individuals can actually change their lives by networking with others about something they were going to do anyway and that is travel. Travel is a seven trillion dollar business worldwide. That speaks volumes on where people are spending their disposable income. People simply love to travel and the proof is in the financial numbers.

Life Changing

Speaking from sheer experience, I can honestly state that YTB has truly been a life-changing experience. My wife and I have gained a viable business, we have generated extra income, and we have formulated great relationships with good people. No one had to tell us twice when we had the opportunity to hear about YTB. Our daughter's God-Father, Robert Wesley, invited my wife and I to an opportunity meeting and my wife was not able to attend, but I proceeded to attend without her. The meeting was interesting, informative and taught by a knowledgeable gentleman by the name of Keenith Reed, who is currently, our Level 1 National Sales Director. The same night as the meeting, I went home and told my wife about the experience and I explained why I felt that she should be in the business. She listened and the rest is history, as they say. We are currently in the business and we are doing quite well. We are common people taking advantage of a great opportunity. YTB can be your dream come true, but you must first dare to dream.

About the Biz

For a mere cost of under $500.00, an individual can purchase a YTB business and become a RTA (Referring Travel Affiliate).

That's right, your own travel biz for less than $500.00 with no annual renewal fees. You must admit that $500.00 is not a lot of money to own a business with a phenomenal company. As one of our high-ranking directors, Spencer Iverson, stated at a presentation in Los Angeles, "If you don't have access to $500.00 to join this business, then your plan 'A' is not working." He definitely said a mouthful that night, and I definitely agreed with him as I still do. Of course there are always exceptions to the rule, but for the most part, people can get a hold of $500.00 if they really need to.

As with any legitimate business, there is an operating cost to do business. In other words, every business has their share of bills, such as water, gas, electric, telephone and other miscellaneous items. Bills are a normal part of doing business. As a YTB business owner, you too have a monthly cost for doing business and it is only $49.95. The fantastic blessing about YTB, is that the company has created an avenue where you are able to recoup your $49.95, each and every month. Essentially, you have the opportunity to operate an overhead-free business as my wife and I do. Once you decide to inquire more about the business, the information will be provided to you regarding operating an overhead free business.

Once you join the YTB family, the world of travel is literally at your fingertips via your online business. You can adhere to your travel desires as well as fulfill the dreams of countless individuals, while making money. Travelocity, who is partnered with YTB, powers your online booking engine. You actually receive two websites once you purchase the business. One is the booking engine as stated earlier and the other website is your virtual secretary better known as your back office. Anything that takes place with your business is tracked by the latter website. Whether it be earnings, sales, new company business, training etc., your virtual secretary keeps a record of all events. It is a paperless experience for you as a business owner.

Your general website is state-of-the-art and is updated in real time whenever new information is introduced by your parent company the YTB Network.

All the familiar vendors that you are accustomed to doing business with will more than likely be present on your website. For instance, rental car vendors, your favorite airline carriers, popular hotels and major cruise lines such as Carnival are present on your website for the taking. You even have your own ticket vendor, called "Tickets Now." This gives you the ability to sell tickets to concerts, musicals, sporting events, including golf packages and hunting/fishing excursions. People can also purchase flowers for all occasions and they can even buy new and used vehicles from your YTB website.

The recent business relationships that have been formed with YTB are exciting. YTB is already elated from their extended relationships with Travelocity and Carnival Cruise Lines. But, now there are other major companies who have joined forces with YTB. The companies are Staples, Dell Computers, Sprint and UPS. I would be willing to bet that there are more companies on the way. It is undeniable when a company is experiencing exponential growth such as YTB, that other businesses are taking immediate notice.

Also, as a YTB Referring Travel Affiliate, you receive 60% of the vendor commissions on all bookings generated on your travel website. The commissions increase to 70% after completing training. And, you receive commissions and bonuses upon referring new travel agents to the business. YTB is constantly rewarding you for your efforts.

As a YTB business owner, you own a home-based business, which allows you to be privy to several tax deductions. It is recommended that you obtain a tax professional who is savvy in home-based businesses, so that you won't miss any eligible deductions.

One of the greatest rewards for being a part of YTB is to be able to purchase stock from your own company, that's amazing. There should be no skepticism about YTB since they are a publicly-traded company. If the security exchange commission has done the research concerning YTB, that is good enough for me.

Last but not least, the YTB founders have formulated an awesome compensation plan for their Referring Travel Agents. You can actually make good money with your business. Matter of fact, some people have made great money from owning a business with YTB. There is even a group of folks in YTB, better known as the **Circle of Champions**, who have become millionaires from their efforts through YTB.

Jerome Hughes & Katrina Greenhill, Steve Branch & T.V. Wilson, Camaron and Jamie Corr, Dave & Marlis Funk, Ron & Judy Head, Bill & Anne Hoffmann, Peter Jensen, Kent & Kim McLaughlin, James & Marcia Prewitt, Rick & Brenda Ricketts, Juliet St. John, Floyd & Carla Williams, and our personal friends, Donald & Deborah Bradley. The latest millionaires to join the rank of Circle of Champions is **Andrew & Chantal Lakey.**

Yes, you can make a great living with YTB, but you do have to put your best foot forward. This is not a get rich quick scheme. To make money you do need to devote some time to your business to become successful.

What To Expect
You might ask, what should you expect after investing $500.00 for a YTB business. From personal experi-

ence, my wife and I can tell you that it is really left up to you regarding the success you wish to obtain with YTB. Only you know the financial level that would be comfortable for you and your family. You really do determine where you would like to be financially in YTB, based on your outcome of work. If you spend minimal time building your business, you will reap small dividends. If you spend adequate time building your business, you will reap good dividends. You set the formula and the stage for your financial future. A couple thousand dollars extra a month may be a great asset to you and your family, while some families will benefit just from an extra couple of hundred dollars a month. And yes, some people are so motivated from the possibilities of their YTB business, that they set their monetary goals at several thousand dollars a month. My wife and I are privileged to be acquainted with many individuals who own YTB businesses and who are making several thousand dollars a month. We are very happy for anyone who has set financial goals with YTB and has actually accomplished them.

Personally, my wife and I have met our initial financial goals within YTB and now we desire to move on to the director level, where you receive a guaranteed monthly salary on top of the many commissions and bonuses that YTB has to offer.

No matter if my wife and I make $200.00 per month in supplemental income; $2,000.00 per month extra income, or even $20,000.00 in additional income, the ultimate goal is to leave residual income for our children to reap.

T & I Should Apply

The 'T' is for tools. While in business, it is incumbent upon your leadership to supply the necessary tools that you need in order to be successful in your business. Without the proper leadership and business tools, your avenue for success may be derailed. The better your leadership, the more realistic your chances are to be successful in business.

The 'I' is for individual. Each individual must do his/her part to ensure his/her own success while in business. You can have the best leadership in the universe, but if you fail to follow your leadership, you will never be able to lead a successful business. Also, you can be presented with the most sophisticated tools to assist you, but if you do not take the initiative to utilize them, you severely stunt your growth in business.

Friends & Family

Once you have begun your YTB business, I am sure that you would want to spread the word to your friends and family. Matter of fact, your friends and family should be the first ones to support your business. Can you imagine having a travel business and your family members book their travel elsewhere? Would that be the ultimate insult? It just doesn't make sense. Your family and friends should be your first line of support. If that is not the case, I vow to you that there is something mysteriously out of place and wrong. Your friends and family members are not who they say they are if you don't garner their support. Shame on your so-called friends and family in the tenth degree if they don't support you.

Charity and goodwill starts at home, but don't be surprised if your biggest support system comes from strangers. I urge you to do the right thing and support small business owners, especially, if they are your friends or family members.

I'm just a common man with a simple plan

Note: Just days before this book was sent to final production, the YTB Network became the largest retail distributor in the world. Over 600 retail stores joined the YTB family. You and your family can now shop at most of your favorite retail stores on your own YTB internet store. **Wow!!!**

Now, I urge you to go take on the world.

**With a YTB business you will experience
the following:**

Own a home-based business under $500 . . . . *YTB.*
Enjoy first class travel . . . .*YTB.*
Generate residual income . . . .*YTB.*
A publicly-traded company . . . .*YTB.*
Phenomenal income potential . . . .*YTB.*
Huge tax deductions . . . .*YTB.*
YTB relationships . . . .*Beyond Priceless.*
The people we have met through YTB have been tremendous mentors and a blessing to have as new friends.

For more information go to: *www.delta4lifetravel.info*
and click on *company presentation*. Or, talk with the
terrific person that referred this book to you.

**In closing, I bid you phenomenal blessings in all that
you do. Remember, I'm just a common man with a
simple plan.**

Back Word

My Why

Yes indeed, my why would make me cry almost on a daily basis. My beautiful baby girl, born totally normal and then the unthinkable happens. She was damaged at the hands of medical professionals. That chapter of my life was so hurtful, so painful that I honestly did not want to go on with life. Yes, it was quite a life-changing experience. I did have a support system in place that was small, but oh so mighty. My mother, Doris, my spiritual moms, Ms. Dorothy, and Granny-Vi, and last but certainly not least my incredible husband, Erick, who was hurting as well. We all prayed for understanding and for guidance to lead us through this difficult journey.

There were days when I thought that God had left me alone to bare this sorrow in my own dark-tunnel. As I managed the strength to pray, I could see through the wetness of my tears that there was a glimmer of light at the end of the tunnel. God was still there, and he yearned for me to reach out to him. There were many days that I was unsuccessful but as time went on, I was able to reach out to Him and He reached back and touched my heart and hugged my spirit. God assured me that He would never leave me nor forsake me. God also revealed to me through prophesy that my daughter Déja will be healed. I stand on God's word and I have faith that He will do what He has revealed in our daughter's health.

Today, I live with the hope of "Great Expectations." I believe my daughter will be healed and I expect to be a National Sales Director with YTB. During my lowest point, God brought YTB into my life as a gift from our good friends Robert and Darcelle Wesley. YTB was the conduit that connected me to a great business as well as some of the most caring people in the entire world. I am honored that God chose me to be affiliated with such an awesome company that is led by true men of faith.

I anticipate great things in the near future. God's word states that, "To whom much is given, much is required." I am truly up for the challenges that are set before me with the comfort of knowing that God directs my path.

My "Why" can make me cry but God's gift of YTB has helped to dry up some of the tears.

By

DeJoiré C. Benson

Do you remember the question presented in the scenario at the beginning of the book? Now is your opportunity to answer the question.

This book was written just for you, and maybe, you will consider chapters 1-10 when making decisions concerning basic business and finances.

The moral of the original question is, only you can answer the scenario, because only you can solve the equation. Just think about it, by you temporarily sacrificing an item, outing, or event, your life could change financially forever.

Family, fun, and finances can be a beautiful combination.

My advice: Always consider the most precious things in life when making important decisions. In addition, always remember to pray.

Erick G. Benson: *A New Age Renaissance Man*

As an accomplished author, playwright and producer, **Erick G. Benson** has become the urban culture's modern-day Renaissance man. Although juggling his family life and a career as a peace officer is not an easy task, Benson does not miss a beat when it comes to fulfilling his passion for creative writing and producing for film and television.

A graduate of California State Polytechnic University, Pomona, Erick G. Benson earned a Bachelor of Science Degree in Communications in 1983. As a student, he worked as a live news camera operator for channel 18 KSCI Global Television and performed post-production duties for various cable TV stations. Upon graduating from the University, he joined the Mark Goodson Production Company as a Public Relations Representative, with the game show staff of **Family Feud**. Next, he demonstrated his advertising skills as an Account Executive with P.D.S. Sports Inc., where he sold radio spots for the company's radio show, *Inside Track*. Erick also worked as an Account Executive with Ted Salter and Associates in conjunction with 1580 KDAY Radio Station in Los Angeles. Soon after, he and an associate formed the Benson & Rosenthal Advertising Agency. As for the popular hit television show, **Love Connection**, Mr. Benson was responsible for promotions and recruitment of contestants throughout Southern California. He also directed a contemporary variety show featuring Grammy award winner, Anita Baker.

In 1992, Benson attended UCLA to further enhance his script writing ability. In July 1993, he wrote a specialized article, which was published nationally in **ESSENCE Magazine**. The article was also featured on **B.E.T.** (Black Entertainment Television) in May and July of 1994.

In February 1995, he wrote and produced the hit stage play, **Sistah Story**, which premiered in Los Angeles at the Wilshire Ebell Theater, and subsequently toured throughout Southern and Northern California.   He has more recently written and directed three additional stage plays: **The Lost Season (1996)**, **The Risen Verdict (1998)** and **Bethlehem on Broadway**, which premiered in **December 2001** at the Ontario Convention Center.

In July 2005, Benson earned a *Masters Degree in Creative Writing*. Since then, he has written several film scripts through the partnership of Ben-Her Entertainment and completed Director and Producer courses through the Hollywood Film Institute.

Benson continued to add to his vast accomplishments in April 2006, when he wrote and produced a sitcom entitled, **First Cousins**, featuring veteran television actor, Sherman Hemsley. The sitcom was embraced by Warner Bros. and forwarded to the CW Network executives and is still in production consideration for the television network.

Benson recently completed his second book entitled, **Framed Justice**, which was released in August 2007. **The Weight-Pile Murder** was the first book he released as a mystery writer. The third book in the trilogy is entitled, **Black White Boy**, which will be completed in 2010.

Benson is the Director of Drama for Loveland Church, which is one of the largest churches in the Inland Empire. .

For more information about Erick Benson, please visit his website: www.urbandreamsfilmworks.com.

Recommended Books

* Lower Your Taxes BIG TIME!– **Sandy Botkin**, CPA, Esq.
* Your First Year in Network Marketing– **Mark Yarnell** & **Rene Reid Yarnell**
* The 45-Second Presentation That Will Change Your Life- **Don Failla**
* Why We Want You to be Rich- **Donald Trump** & **Robert Kiyosaki**
* Think and Grow Rich- **Napoleon Hill**
* The Automatic Millionaire- **David Bach**
* Smart Couples Finish Rich- **David Bach**
* How to Start a Conversation and Make Friends- **Don Gabor**
* How to Win Friends and Influence People- **Dale Carnegie**
* The 360E Leader- **John Maxwell**
* Developing the Leader Within You- **John Maxwell**
* DRIVEN FROM WITHIN- **Michael Jordan**
* A Year of Growing Rich, 52 Steps to Achieving Life's Rewards-**Napoleon Hill**
* The ABCs of MAKING MONEY – **Dr. Denis Cauvier** and **Alan Lysaght**
* THE WALK TO WEALTH- 7 Guiding Principles to Prosperity - **Andria Hall**
* THE 3 CEOs *formula* For Building Success & Wealth in Network Marketing and Life-**Spencer Iverson, Donald Bradley, Floyd Williams**

About the Author

Erick G. Benson has been published nationally in Essence magazine and his work has been featured on B.E.T. (Black Entertainment Television). Mr. Benson has a B.S. Degree in Communications and a M.A. Degree in Creative Writing. Also, he has over 19 years of experience in law enforcement and he currently works with the Department of Corrections as a Parole Agent.

Printed in the United States
210597BV00001B/1-126/P